FRESH DESIGNS
MEN

FEATURING DESIGNS BY

Amy Duncan
Erica Jackofsky
Jenna Swanson
Karen Bourquin
Katherine Vaughan
Nikki Adams
Rebekah Bromwell
Ruth Garcia-Alcantud
Stephannie Tallent
Susanna Ferguson

AND PHOTOGRAPHY BY

Robert Gladys / Fractured Photography

COOPERATIVE PRESS
Cleveland, OH
cooperativepress.com

FRESH DESIGNS: MEN

ISBN 13: 978-0-9792017-9-0
First Edition
Published by Cooperative Press
http://www.cooperativepress.com

Patterns © 2012, their designers, as credited
Photos © 2012, Robert Gladys, Fractured Photography (fracturedphotography.com) except page 6 by Erica Jackofsky

Makeup by Elle Gemma, Spell Cosmetics (spellcosmetics.com)
Models: Arabella Proffer, Ben Vendetta, Chris McKay

Every effort has been made to ensure that all the information in this book is accurate at the time of publication, however Cooperative Press neither endorses nor guarantees the content of external links referenced in this book.

If you have questions or comments about this book, or need information about licensing, custom editions, special sales, or academic/corporate purchases, please contact Cooperative Press: info@cooperativepress.com or 13000 Athens Ave C288, Lakewood, OH 44107 USA

No part of this book may be reproduced in any form, except brief excerpts for the purpose of review, without prior written permission of the publisher. Thank you for respecting our copyright.

FOR COOPERATIVE PRESS

Senior Editor: Shannon Okey
Assistant Editor: Elizabeth Green Musselman
Developmental Editor: Abra Forman
Technical Editor: Alexandra Virgiel
Production Manager: MJ Kim
With additional assistance by Sarah Jo Burch

TABLE OF CONTENTS

AMY DUNCAN	Cooper Scarf	(page 5)
ERICA JACKOFSKY	Rhythm Maker's Hat	(page 7)
JENNA SWANSON	Bäume Socks	(page 11)
KAREN BOURQUIN	Gone Fishin' Sweater	(page 15)
KATHERINE VAUGHAN	Sartor Vest	(page 19)
NIKKI ADAMS	Stairway Sweater	(page 25)
REBEKAH BROMWELL	Brick Stitch Scarf	(page 29)
RUTH GARCIA-ALCANTUD	Brian Cardigan	(page 31)
STEPHANNIE TALLENT	Abalone Cove Hat	(page 37)
SUSANNA FERGUSON	Riga Sweater	(page 41)

ACKNOWLEDGMENTS (page 44)
ABOUT COOPERATIVE PRESS AND THE FRESH DESIGNS SERIES (page 45)

ABBREVIATIONS (page 46)

COOPER SCARF
BY AMY DUNCAN

EASY

Keeping warm has never been so cool as with this elegant scarf with a hip steampunk edge. Wear it as a loose cowl for a night out or buttoned up with functional sleek and stylish hardware and with your best leather to keep you warm. The possibilities are endless with this aviator-on-its-head scarf.

SIZE
One size

FINISHED MEASUREMENTS
Width: 7"/18cm
Length: 50"/127cm

MATERIALS
Pigeonroof Studios Cassiopeia DK [75% merino wool, 15% cashmere, 10% silk; 260yd/238m per 100g skein]; color Bitter Orange; 2 skeins

1 set US #6/4mm straight needles

Six 5/8"/16mm heavy duty brass snaps (Dritz 981-38)
Snap install tool or rubber mallet

GAUGE
24 sts/32 rows = 4"/10cm in stockinette
26 sts/32 rows = 4"/10cm in pattern

PATTERN
Cast on 40 sts.
Row 1: Sl1, *p1, k1; rep from * to last 2 sts, k2.
Row 2: Sl1, *k1, p1; rep from * to last 2 sts, k2.
Row 3: Rep Row 1.
Row 4: Rep Row 2.
Row 5 [RS]: Sl1, p1, k1, p1, *sl1 pwise wyif, k1; rep from * to last 4 sts, k1, p1, k2.
Row 6 [WS]: Sl1, k1, p1, k1, purl to last 3 sts, k1, p2.
Row 7: Sl1, p1, k1, p1, *k1, sl1 pwise wyif; rep from * to last 4 sts, k1, p1, k2.
Row 8: Rep Row 6.
Repeat Rows 5–8 until scarf measures 49"/125cm or desired length, then work Rows 1–4 again. Bind off loosely.

FINISHING
Weave in ends. Block to desired dimensions and drape.

Using a snap install tool or rubber mallet on a solid surface, install the snaps along the border approximately 3.5"/9cm apart (see photo for placement). Make sure to install the two parts of the snaps so that the scarf can be snapped closed into an untwisted loop.

ABOUT THE DESIGNER
Amy Duncan began knitting in 2007, and soon the dining room was covered in yarns, patterns, and blocking squares. You can find her at http://www.TwoSticksandaSheep.com and on Ravelry and Twitter as Duncks.

RHYTHM MAKER'S HAT

BY ERICA JACKOFSKY

INTERMEDIATE

This design was inspired by Chris, the rhythm maker in my life. Wear it as he does with the ribbing unrolled for a casual slouch hat, or try folding the brim up for a more classic fitting beanie.

SIZE
Child [Men's, Big Men's]
Shown in Men's size

FINISHED MEASUREMENTS
Circumference: 16.5 [20, 23]"/42 [51, 58.5]cm
Remember that hats should fit with at least 2"/5cm (and up to 4"/10cm) of negative ease to stay securely in place.

MATERIALS
Three Irish Girls Springvale Super Merino [100% merino wool; 230 yds/210 m per 100g skein]; 1 [1, 1] skein. Shown in Murphy (dark brown) and Brennan (medium brown).

16"/40cm US #5/3.75mm circular needle
16"/40cm US #6/4mm circular needle
1 set US #6/4mm double-point needles

4 stitch markers

GAUGE
24 sts/30 rnds = 4"/10cm in k2, p2 rib, slightly stretched using smaller needles
22 sts/28 rnds = 4"/10cm in stockinette on larger needles

STITCH INSTRUCTIONS
Chevron Weave Pattern (multiple of 10 sts)
Rnd 1 and all odd-numbered rnds: Knit.
Rnd 2: *K2, sl3 wyif, k2, sl3 wyif; rep from * to end.
Rnd 4: *Sl1 wyif, k2, sl3 wyif, k2, sl2 wyif; rep from * to end.
Rnd 6: *Sl2 wyif, k2, sl3 wyif, k2, sl1 wyif; rep from * to end.
Rnd 8: *Sl3 wyif, k2, sl3 wyif, k2; rep from * to end.
Rnd 10: *K1, sl3 wyif, k2, sl3 wyif, k1; rep from* to end.
Rnd 12: *K2, sl3 wyif, k2, sl3 wyif; rep from * to end.
Rnd 14: *K1, sl3 wyif, k2, sl3 wyif, k1; rep from * to end.
Rnd 16: *Sl3 wyif, k2, sl3 wyif, k2; rep from * to end.
Rnd 18: *Sl2 wyif, k2, sl3 wyif, k2, sl1 wyif; rep from * to end.
Rnd 20: *Sl1 wyif, k2, sl3 wyif, k2, sl2 wyif; rep from * to end.

PATTERN NOTES
This pattern is offered with both written-out and charted instructions, including full charts for the crown decreases.

PATTERN
Using smaller needles, cast on 100 [120, 140] sts. Pm and join for working in the rnd. Work in k2, p2 rib for 3 [4, 4]"/7.5 [10, 10]cm. Change to larger needles.

Work Rnds 1–20 of Chevron Weave patt 1 [2, 2] times, then Rnds 1–10 another 1 [0, 0] times.

Crown Decreases
Rnd 1: (K25 [30, 35], pm) 4 times.
Rnd 2: (K1, ssk, work in pattern to 3 sts before marker, k2tog, k1, sl marker) 4 times. 8 sts dec'd.
Rnd 3: Knit.
Rep Rnds 2–3 twice more, then Rnd 2 only until 20 [24, 20] sts remain.

Sizes Child and Big Men's only:
Next rnd: (Ssk, k1, k2tog) 4 times. 12 sts.
Next rnd: (Sl2, k1, pass 2 sl sts over) 4 times. 4 sts.

Size Men's only:
Next rnd: (K1, ssk, k2tog, k1) 4 times. 16 sts.
Next rnd: (Ssk, k2tog) 4 times. 8 sts.

FINISHING
Cut yarn and pull through remaining 4 [8, 4] sts.
Fasten off & weave in ends.
Block as necessary.

MAIN CHART

CHILD CHART

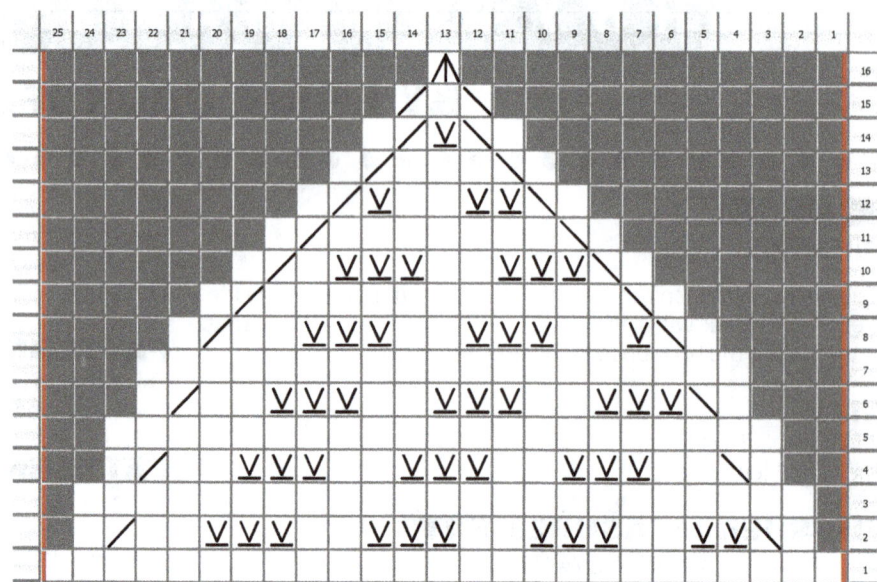

MEN'S CHART

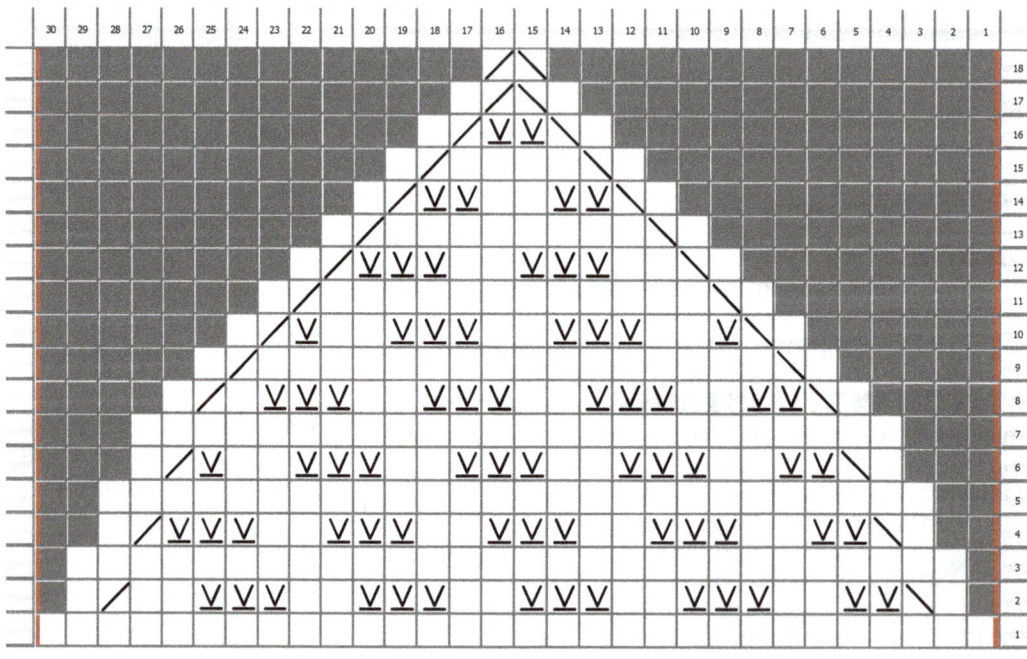

BIG MEN'S CHART

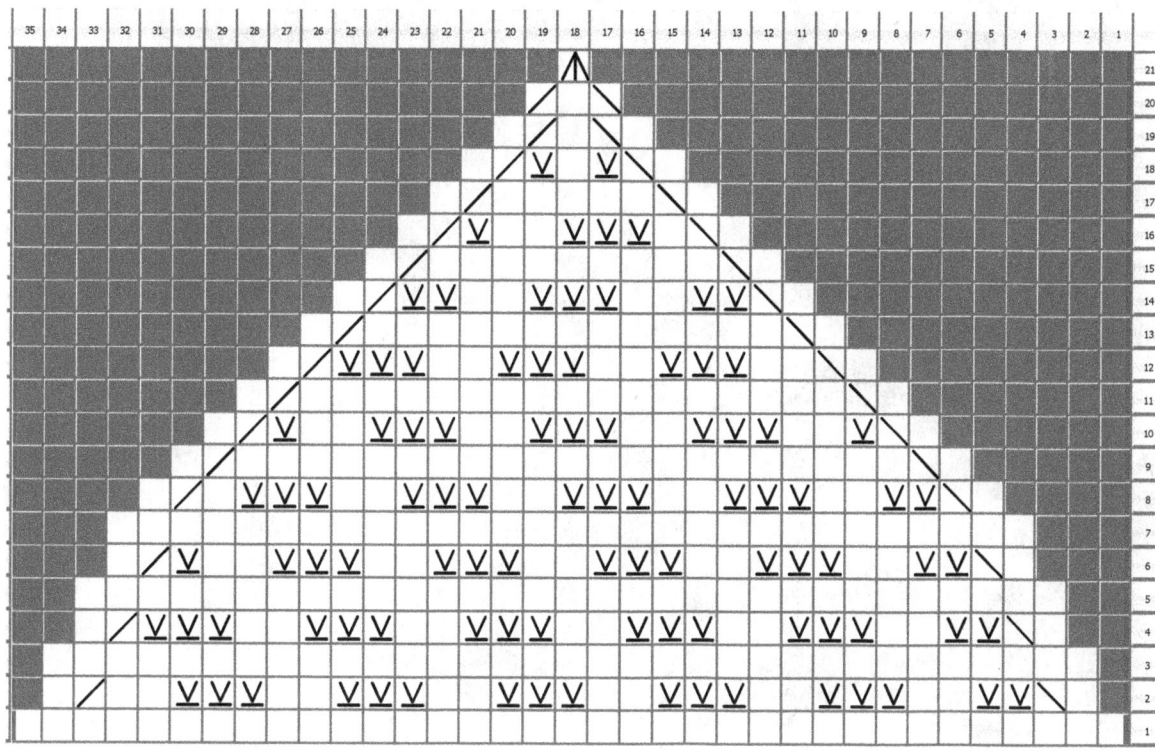

ABOUT THE DESIGNER
Erica spends her time fiddling around the country with The Homegrown String Band. Knitting keeps her sane on the seemingly endless hours of travel time to gigs. You can find Erica online at FiddleKnits.com, or on Ravelry as FiddleKnitsDesign.

knit
knit stitch

No Stitch
Placeholder - No stitch made.

ssk
Slip one stitch as if to knit, Slip another stitch as if to knit. Insert left-hand needle into front of these 2 stitches and knit them together

slip wyif
Slip stitch as if to purl, with yarn in front

k2tog
Knit two stitches together as one stitch

Central Double Dec
Slip first and second stitches together as if to knit. Knit 1 stitch. Pass two slipped stitches over the knit stitch.

BÄUME SOCKS

BY JENNA SWANSON

INTERMEDIATE

These socks were inspired by my brother and father-in-law's frequent treks in the woods. The cable rib pattern reminds me of the intertwining branches of trees in the forest. The socks feature a long cuff, and are knit in a squishy, worsted-weight yarn. Because of the thick yarn, they knit up surprisingly quickly, making them ideal for gift giving.

SIZE
S [L]
Shown in size L

FINISHED MEASUREMENTS
Foot circumference (unstretched): 7.5 [9]"/19 [23]cm
Length: Custom

MATERIALS
Three Irish Girls Springvale Super Merino [100% merino wool; 230 yd/229m per 100g skein]; color Brennan; 2 [2] skeins

1 set US #5/3.75mm double pointed needles

Stitch marker
Cable needle (cn)

GAUGE
20 sts/28 rows = 4"/10cm in stockinette
24 sts/26 rows = 4"/10cm in pattern

PATTERN
Cuff
Cast on 40 [48] sts using the long-tail cast on and join to work in the round, being careful not to twist.
Work the 12 rnds of Chart four times.

Heel Flap
Heel flap is worked over 20 [24] sts. Leave the instep sts on a holder or spare needle.
Row 1 [RS)]: (Sl1, k1) 10 [12] times, turn.
Row 2 [WS]: Sl1, p19 [23].
Rep Rows 1–2 until heel flap measures 3"/8.5cm, ending with Row 2.

Turn Heel
Row 1 [RS]: Sl1, k10 [12], ssk, k1, turn.
Row 2 [WS]: Sl1, p3, p2tog, p1, turn.
Row 3: Sl1, k4, ssk, k1, turn.
Row 4: Sl1, p5, p2tog, p1, turn.
Continue as set by last 2 rows, working 1 more st before the dec on each succeeding row, until all heel flap sts have been used up. RS should be facing for next row.

Gusset
Knit across the 12 [14] rem heel sts, then pick up and knit 13 sts from side of heel flap. This is needle 1. Resume working chart over held instep sts. This is needle 2. Pick up and knit 13 sts from other side of heel flap, and with the same needle, knit 6 [7] heel sts from needle 1. This is needle 3.
You should have 19 [20] stitches on needles 1 and 3, and 20 [24] stitches on needle 2. The round begins at the center of the heel.

Rnd 1: Knit to 3 sts before end of needle 1, k2tog, k1; work in pattern across needle 2; on needle 3, k1, ssk, knit to end. 2 sts dec'd.
Rnd 2: Knit across needle 1, work in patt across needle 2, knit across needle 3.
Rep Rnds 1–2 until 10 [12] sts remain on needles 1 and 3 and 20 [24] sts remain on needle 2. 40 [48] sts in total.

Foot
Work even, with sole in stockinette and instep in pattern, until foot measures 2"/5cm less than desired finished length.

Toe
Rnd 1: Knit to 3 sts before end of needle 1, k2tog, k1; on needle 2, k1, ssk, knit to 3 sts before end, k2tog, k1; on needle 3, k1, ssk, knit to end. 4 sts dec'd.
Rnd 2: Knit.
Rep Rnds 1–2 until 16 sts rem.
Knit sts from needle 1 onto needle 3.
Graft (Kitchener st) the toe closed.

FINISHING
Weave in ends. Block if desired.

ABOUT THE DESIGNER
Jenna enjoys designing patterns that fit the gap between beginner knits and complicated patterns. Her favorite garments to design are socks and boy's sweaters. She is getting used to knitting and living in Texas. Jenna blogs here: www.gidgetstitches.com, and can be found on Ravelry as Gidgettm.

knit
knit stitch

purl
purl stitch

Left Twist, purl bg
sl1 to CN, hold in front. p1. k1 from CN

Right Twist, purl bg
sl1 to CN, hold in back. k1, p1 from CN

Left Twist
sl1 to CN, hold in front. k1, k1 from CN

GONE FISHIN' SWEATER
BY KAREN BOURQUIN

INTERMEDIATE

A weekend away fishing or just relaxing at a cottage was the inspiration for this sweater. Relaxed shaping that combines moss stitch columns with vertical cables, knit in a yarn that provides terrific stitch definition, that is perfect for any season.

SIZE
S-M [L-XL, 2XL]
Shown in size S-M

FINISHED MEASUREMENTS
Chest: 44 [48.5, 53.75]"/112 [123, 136]cm
Length: 26.25 [27.25, 28.25]"/66.5 [69, 72]cm

MATERIALS
Hemp for Knitting Hempton [40% cotton, 30% hemp, 30 % modal; 130yd/120m per 50g skein]; color #066 Cypress; 24 [28, 30] skeins

32"/80cm US #7/4.5mm circular needle
16"/40cm US #7/4.5mm circular needle

Stitch holders
Stitch marker

GAUGE
15 sts/24 rows = 4"/10cm in stockinette with yarn doubled
18 sts/24 rows = 4"/10cm in pattern with yarn doubled

PATTERN NOTES
This sweater is knit flat in pieces and seamed. The yarn is held double throughout.

PATTERN
Back
With 2 strands of yarn held together and longer needle, cast on 90 [100, 110] sts. Work 4 rows stockinette, beg with a knit row.
Next row [RS]: Knit, inc 11 [11, 13] sts evenly spaced. 101 [111, 123] sts
Knit 1 row. Purl 1 row.
Pattern set-up row [WS]: K2 [7, 2], work Body Chart (beg with Row 2) to last 2 [7, 2] sts, knit to end.
Pattern set-up row [RS]: P2 [7, 2], work Body Chart to last 2 [7, 2] sts, purl to end.
Continue as set by last 2 rows until piece measures 23 [24, 25]"/58.5 [61, 63.5]cm, ending with a WS row.

Shape neck
Next row [RS]: Work 34 [38, 43] sts in patt, join second ball of yarn and bind off center 33 [35, 37] sts, work in patt to end.
Working each side separately, dec 1 st at neck edge on next row and foll WS row. 32 [36, 41] sts rem each side.
Work even until piece measures 24 [25, 26]"/61 [63.5, 66]cm. Bind off.

Front
Work same as Back until piece measures 22.5 [23.5, 24.5]"/57 [59.5, 62]cm, ending with a WS row.

Shape neck
Next row [RS]: Work 34 [38, 43] sts in patt, k2tog, join second ball of yarn and bind off center 29 [31, 33] sts, ssk, work to end in patt. 35 [39, 44] sts each side.
Working each side separately, dec 1 st at neck edge on every RS row 3 times. 32 [36, 41] sts rem each side.
Work even until piece measures 24 [25, 26]"/61 [63.5, 66]cm. Bind off.

Sleeves
With 2 strands of yarn held together and longer needle, cast on 40 [42, 44] sts. Work 4 rows in stockinette, beg with a knit row.
Next row [RS]: Knit, inc 5 sts evenly spaced. 45 [47, 49] sts.
Knit 1 row. Purl 1 row.
Pattern set-up row [WS]: K8 [9, 10], work Sleeve Chart (beg with Row 2), k8 [9, 10].
Pattern set-up row [RS]: P8 [9, 10], work Sleeve Chart, p8 [9, 10].

Continuing as set by last 2 rows, inc 1 st at each end on every 6th row 13 [8, 2] times, then every 4th row 7 [14, 23] times. 85 [91, 99] sts. Work all increased sts in reverse stockinette.
Work even until sleeve measures 22"/56cm, ending with a WS row.
Shape saddle

Bind off 31 [34, 38] sts at beg of next 2 rows. 23 sts rem. Work even in patt until saddle measures 7 [8, 9]"/18 [20.5, 23]cm. Place sts on holder.

FINISHING
Block pieces to schematic measurements. Note that schematic measurements are before seaming—1-st selvages are included. Sew saddles to front and back shoulder edges. Sew sleeves to body pieces. Sew side and sleeve underarm seams, reversing seam for rolled edges on sleeves and body.

Collar
With shorter needle and 2 strands of yarn held together, beg at left side of front neckline, pick up and knit 39 [41, 43] sts across front neck, knit sts of right saddle, pick up and knit 37 [39, 41] sts across back neck, knit sts of left saddle. 122 [126, 130] sts. Pm and join to work in the round. Next rnd: Knit, dec 8 sts evenly spaced around. 114 [118, 122] sts. Knit 1 rnd. Purl 2 rnds. Knit 4 rnds. Bind off loosely.

Weave in ends.

ABOUT THE DESIGNER
Karen considers herself fortunate to live on a Pacific Northwest Island where inspiration for designing and necessity for knitted garments combine to make a perfect knitter's environment. Find her online at http://docksideknits.wordpress.com and as oceangrl on Ravelry.

c3 over 3 right
RS: sl3 to CN, hold in back. k3, then k3 from CN
WS: none defined

knit
RS: knit stitch
WS: purl stitch

purl
RS: purl stitch
WS: knit stitch

knit tbl
RS: Knit stitch through back loop
WS: Purl stitch through back loop

c3 over 3 left
RS: sl3 to CN, hold in front. k3, k3 from CN

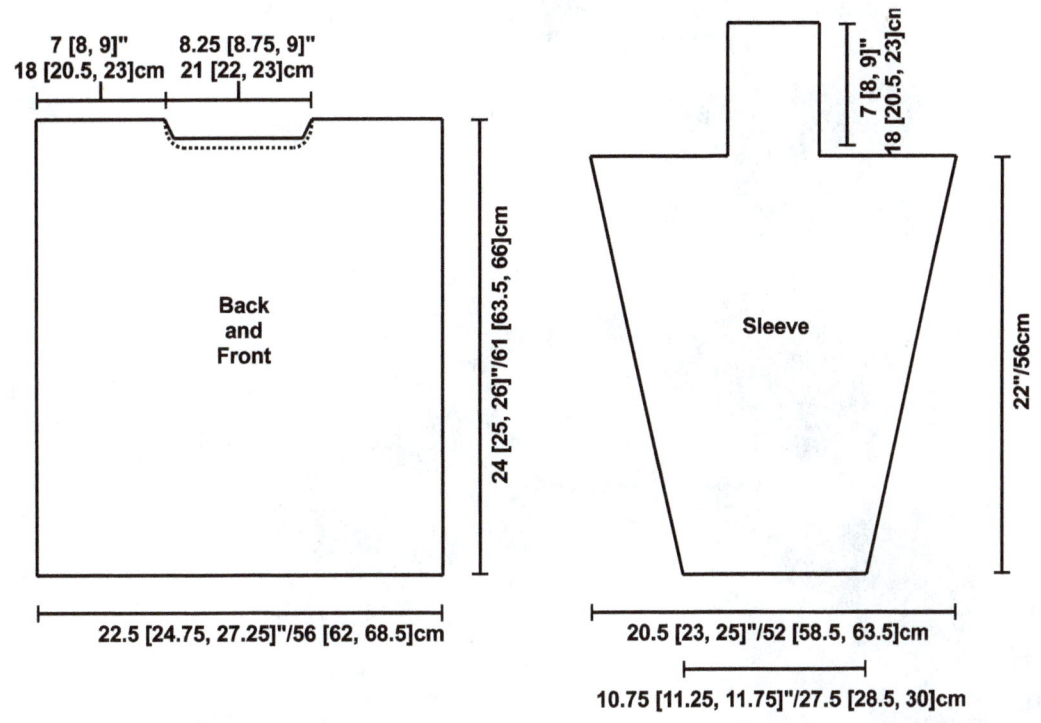

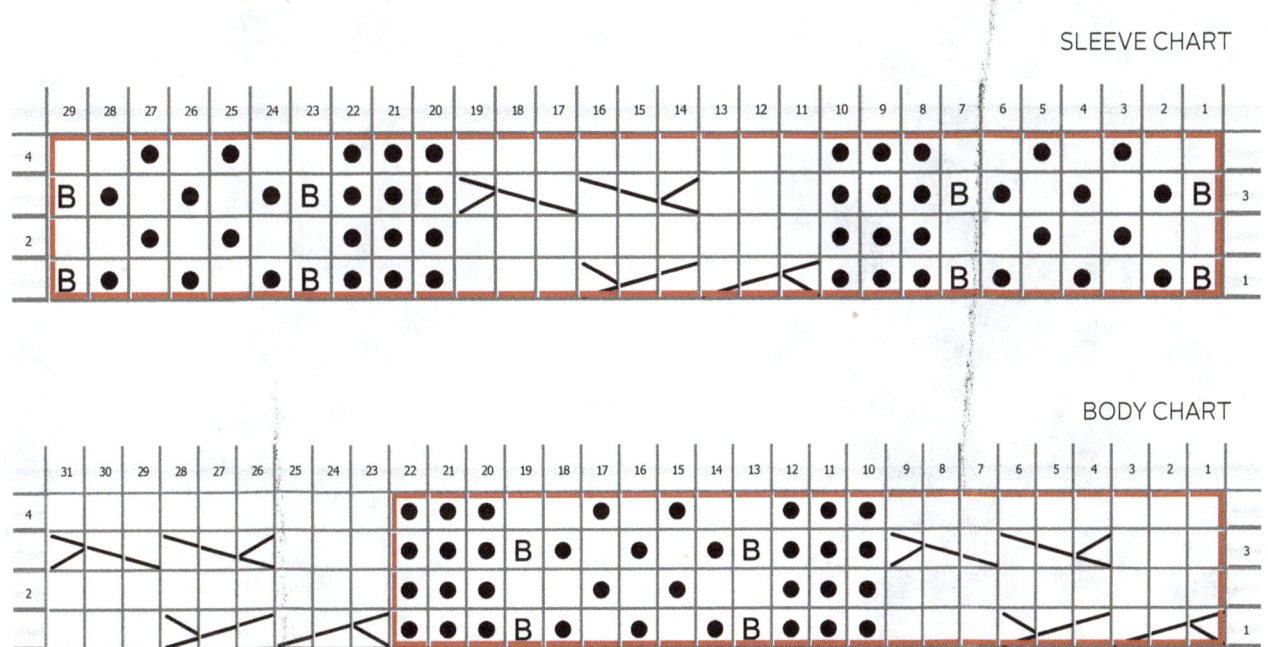

SLEEVE CHART

BODY CHART

SARTOR VEST

BY KATHERINE VAUGHAN

INTERMEDIATE

Men look so dapper and tailored in a knit cabled vest, but many designs seem to have gotten stuck in a "cable up the front" standard layout. This version is modeled on a saddle-shoulder sweater template, with additional panels in the sides that echo the cabled shoulders. Ribbing in the body slims the silhouette while drawing the eye up past the v-neckline and to his handsome face.

SIZE
S [M, L, XL, 2XL]
Shown in size M

FINISHED MEASUREMENTS
Chest: 39.25 [42, 47.5, 50.25, 53]"/99.5 [106.5, 120.5, 127.5, 135]cm
Length: 24.75 [25.25, 26.25, 26.75, 27.25]"/63 [64, 66.5, 68, 69]cm

MATERIALS
Ambrosia and Bliss Amelia Worsted [100% superwash merino wool;
270 yd/247m per 100g skein]; color Sea After a Storm; 3 [4, 4, 5, 5] skeins

1 set US #7/4.5mm straight needles

Cable needle (cn)
Large stitch holder or waste yarn

GAUGE
23 sts/28 rows = 4"/10cm in 2x2 Rib, blocked

PATTERN NOTES
Cabled sections are charted separately. Note the difference between the left and right panels is in the center cable crosses; the left side cables twist to the right while the right side cables twist to the left.

STITCH INSTRUCTIONS
2X2 Rib (multiple of 4 sts + 2)
Row 1 [WS]: P2, *k2, p2; rep from * to end.
Row 2 [RS]: K2, *p2, k2; rep from * to end.
Rep Rows 1–2.

C2/2L (Cable 2 over 2 left): Sl2 to cn and hold in front, k2, k2 from cn.
C2/1Lp (Cable 2 over 1 left purl): Sl2 to cn and hold in front, p1, k2 from cn.
C2/1Rp (Cable 1 over 1 right purl): Sl1 to cn and hold in back, k2, p1 from cn.

SSP (Slip, slip, purl together): Sl 2 sts pwise. Transfer them back to the left needle as they lie. P2tog tbl.

PATTERN
Back
Cast on 86 [94, 110, 118, 126] sts. Work in 2x2 Rib for 14.5 [14.5, 15, 15, 15]"/37 [37, 38, 38, 38]cm, ending with a WS row.

Shape armholes
Row 1 [RS]: K2, p2tog, ssk, *p2, k2; rep from * to last 8 sts, p2, k2tog, p2tog, k2. 4 sts dec'd

Rows 2 and 4 [WS]: Knit the knit sts and purl the purl sts.

Row 3: K2, p1, ssk, p1, *k2, p2; rep from * to last 8 sts, k2, p1, k2tog, p1, k2. 2 sts dec'd.

Row 5: K2, p2tog, p1, *k2, p2; rep from * to last 7 sts, k2, p1, p2tog, k2. 78 [86, 102, 110, 118] sts.

Work even in rib until armholes measure 7.5 [8, 8.5, 9, 9.5]"/19 [20.5, 21.5, 23, 24.5]cm, ending with a WS row.

Shape shoulders
Bind off 8 [8, 9, 10, 10] sts in pattern at beg of next 6 rows. 30 [38, 48, 50, 58] sts rem.
Bind off all rem sts in pattern.

Front
Work as for Back until armholes measure 3.5 [4, 4, 4, 4.5]"/9 [10, 10, 10, 11.5]cm, ending with a WS row.

Shape neck
Row 1 [RS]: Work in est patt across first 36 [40, 48, 52, 56] sts, C2/1Lp, C2/1Rp, work in patt to end.
Row 2 [WS]: Knit the knit sts and purl the purl sts.
Row 3: Work in pattern across first 36 [40, 48, 52, 56] sts, p1, C2/2L, p1, work in pattern to end of row.

Right side:
Row 4 [WS]: Work in pattern across first 31 [35, 43, 47, 51] sts, p2tog, p1, k1, k2tog, p2, turn. Put rem unworked sts on a holder or waste yarn. 37 [41, 49, 53, 57] sts.
Row 5 [RS]: K2, p2, ssk, work in pattern to end. 1 st dec'd.
Row 6: Work in patt to last 6 sts, ssp, k2, p2. 1 st dec'd.
Cont to dec 1 st at neck edge on every row until 24 [24, 27, 30, 30] sts rem.
Work even until armhole measures 7.5 [8, 8.5, 9, 9.5]"/19 [20.5, 21.5, 23, 24.5]cm, ending with a RS row.
Bind off 8 [8, 9, 10, 10] sts in pattern at beg of next three WS rows.

Left side:
Replace held sts on needles. Join new yarn at neck edge with WS facing.
Row 4 [WS]: P2, ssk, k1, p1, ssp, work in pattern to end of row.
Row 5 [RS]: Work in patt to last 6 sts, k2tog, p2, k2.
Row 6: P2, k2, p2tog, work in patt to end.
Cont to dec 1 st at neck edge on every row until 24 [24, 27, 30, 30] sts rem.
Work even until armhole measures 7.5 [8, 8.5, 9, 9.5]"/19 [20.5, 21.5, 23, 24.5]cm, ending with a WS row.
Bind off 8 [8, 9, 10, 10] sts in pattern at beg of next three RS rows.

Shoulder Panels (make 2, Right and Left)
Cast on 20 sts.
Rows 1 and 3 [WS]: P1, k2, *p2, k2; rep from * to last st, p1.
Row 2 [RS]: K1, p2, *k2, p2; rep from * to last st, k1.
Work Rows 1–26 of appropriate Shoulder Chart once, then rep Rows 1–2 of Chart until panel measures 4.25 [4.25, 4.75, 5.25, 5.25]"/11 [11, 12, 13.5, 13.5]cm from cast on. Bind off in pattern.

Side Panels (make 2, Right and Left)
Cast on 30 sts. Work in 2x2 Rib for 1 [1, 1.25, 1.25]"/2.5 [2.5, 3, 3]cm, ending with a WS row.
Work Rows 1–34 of appropriate Side Chart twice, then work Rows 1–2 once more.

Work even in 2x2 Rib until side panel measures 14.5 [14.5, 15, 15, 15]"/37 [37, 38, 38, 38]cm from cast on.
BO all sts in pattern.

FINISHING
Block all pieces to schematic measurements. Note that schematic measurements are before seaming—1-st selvages are included.

Sew side panels to sides of front and back. Sew shoulder panels to top of front and back. Be careful to place panels on correct sides so that the crosses move from front to back.

Weave in ends.

ABOUT THE DESIGNER
Katherine Vaughan has been knitting for 25-plus years and designing for more than five. She primarily designs childrenswear and accessories for adults and the home. As a member of the PhatFiber community she is lucky to have access to excellent handspun and hand-dyed yarns to design with. Katherine daylights as a medical librarian in North Carolina. Find her on the web at http://www.ktlvdesigns.com and on Ravelry as KTLV.

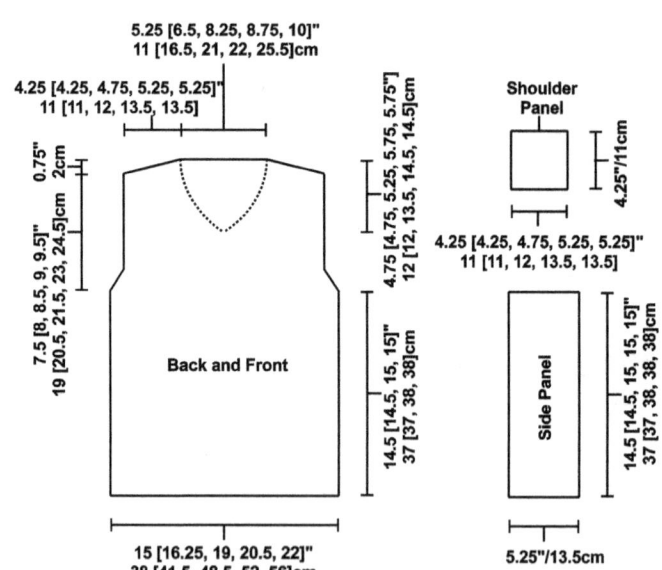

LEFT SHOULDER

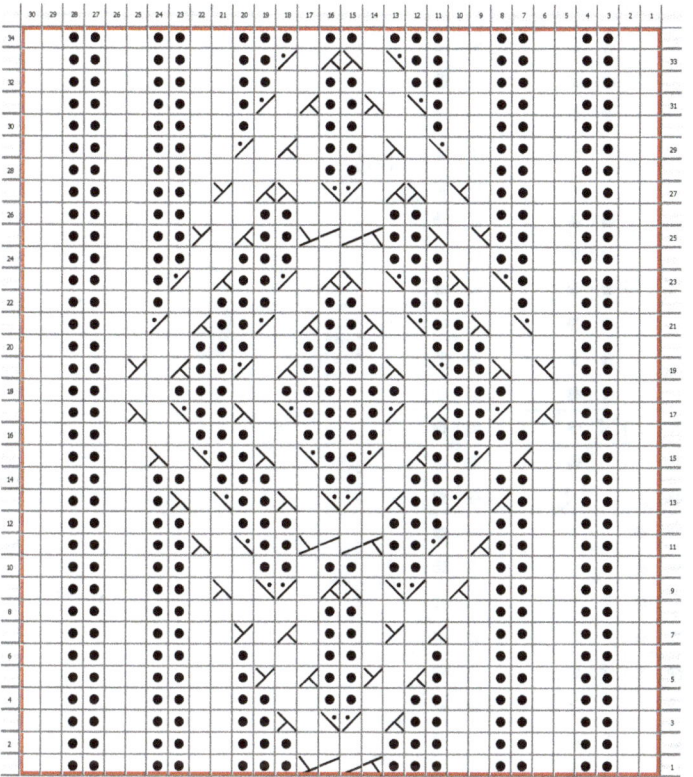

RIGHT SHOULDER

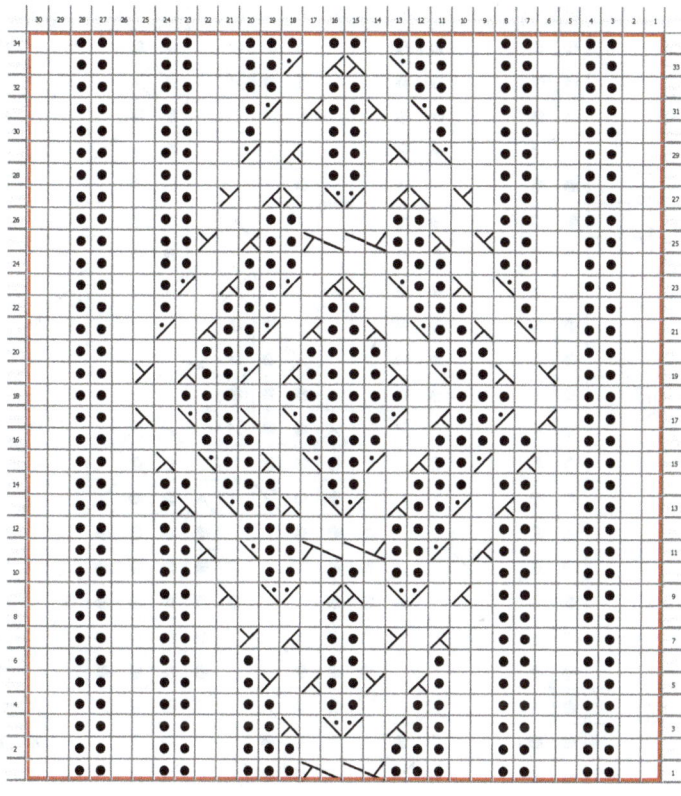

	knit
☐	RS: knit stitch WS: purl stitch

	purl
⬤	RS: purl stitch WS: knit stitch

	c2 over 2 right
	RS: sl2 to CN, hold in back. k2, k2 from CN WS: none defined

	c2 over 1 right P
	RS: sl1 to CN, hold in back. k2, p1 from CN WS: sl1 to CN, hold in back. k2, p1 from CN

	c2 over 1 left P
	RS: sl2 to CN, hold in front. p1, k2 from CN WS: sl2 to CN, hold in front. p1, k2 from CN

	c2 over 1 right
	RS: sl1 to CN, hold in back. k2, k1 from CN WS: sl1 to CN, hold in back. k2, k1 from CN

	c2 over 1 left
	RS: sl2 to CN, hold in front. k1, k2 from CN WS: sl2 to CN, hold in front. k1, k2 from CN

	c2 over 2 left
	RS: sl 2 to CN, hold in front. k2, k2 from CN WS: none defined

LEFT SIDE PANEL

RIGHT SIDE PANEL

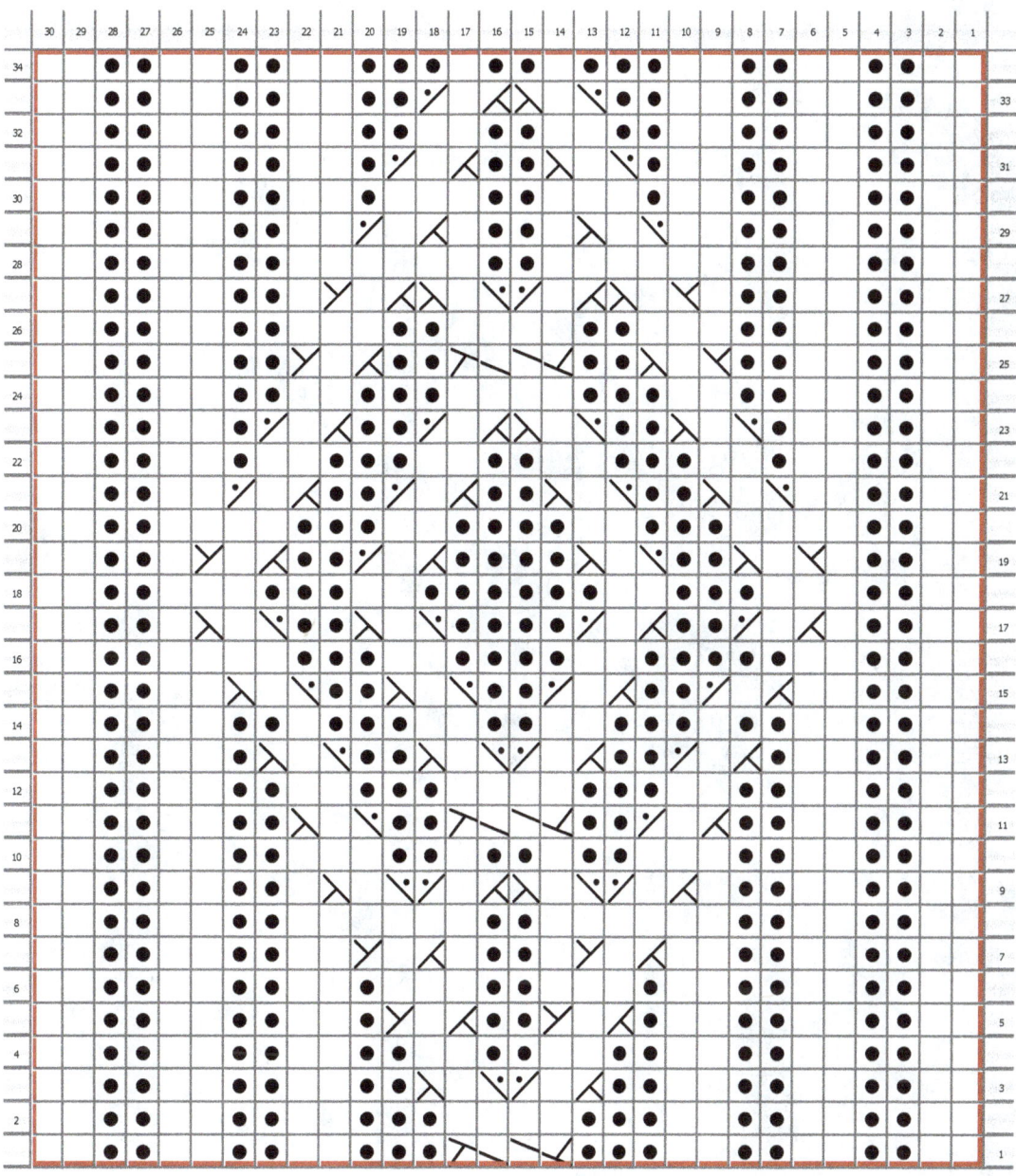

STAIRWAY SWEATER

BY NIKKI ADAMS

EXPERIENCED

It can be a difficult compromise to find a knit that retains its masculinity while not boring the knitter to tears. The garter rib and simple color work in this sweater keep you entertained, and the toned-down colors won't overwhelm the guy wearing it.

SIZE
S [M, L, XL, 2XL]
Shown in size M

FINISHED MEASUREMENTS
Chest: 38.5 [41.25, 44, 46.75, 49.5]"/98 [105, 112, 119, 126]cm
Length: 26.25 [27.25, 27.5, 28, 29]"/66.5 [69, 69.5, 71, 74]cm

Choose a size that is 1–4"/2.5–10cm larger than actual chest measurement.

MATERIALS
[MC] Pigeonroof Studios Superwash Merino [100% superwash merino; 230 yd per 100g skein]; color Charcoal; 6 [6, 7, 8, 9] skeins
[CC1] Pigeonroof Studios Superwash Merino; color Tallow; 1 [1, 1, 1, 1] skeins
[CC2] Pigeonroof Studios Superwash Merino; color undyed; 1 [1, 1, 1, 1] skeins

40"/100cm US #4/3.5mm circular needle

3 stitch markers
Waste yarn

GAUGE
20 sts/28 rows = 4"/10cm in garter rib, blocked

PATTERN NOTES
Back, front, and sleeves are knit flat in separate pieces to the underarm, then joined and the yoke knitted in one piece to the neck. The pattern includes edge stitches throughout. The edge stitches are always worked in stockinette and should not be counted in the rib pattern.

STITCH INSTRUCTIONS
Garter Rib (multiple of 7 sts + 5)
Row 1 [WS]: *P5, k2; rep from * to last 5 sts, p5.
Row 2 [RS]: Knit.
Rep Rows 1–2.

Vertical Stripe Pattern
Stripes are worked in intarsia, in garter stitch (knit every row) and in the garter st portions ("valleys") of the rib. Stripe pattern begins in last 3 garter stitch valleys on the left (as seen with the right side of the piece facing you), beginning with the first stripe as a CC2 stripe. Stripe pattern alternates one CC1, one CC2 stripe. The first (leftmost) stripe will be only 12 rows, the second 24, and from the third on, 36. These first three stripes will be started on the fourth row after the bottom 2x2 rib. From then on, each new stripe is begun to the right 12 rows after the previous one started. The placement of the first few stripes is shown on the chart on page 27.

PATTERN
Front
Cast on 96 [104, 112, 116, 124] sts.
Rows 1–14: *K2, p2; rep from * to end.
Row 15 [RS]: Knit, inc 2 [1, 0, 3, 2] sts evenly across. 98 [105, 112, 119, 126] sts.
Row 16 [WS]: P1 (edge st), work Row 1 of garter rib to last st, p1 (edge st).
Row 17: Knit.

Begin stripe pattern as described in Stitch Instructions. Continue working in garter rib until Front measures 18 [18, 18, 18.5, 19]"/45.5 [45.5, 45.5, 47, 48.5]cm from cast on, ending with a WS row.
Bind off 8 [8, 8, 10, 10] sts at the beg of next two rows. 82 [89, 96, 99, 106] sts. Put sts on waste yarn and set aside.

Back
Work same as Front, omitting color stripe pattern.

Sleeves
CO 60 [60, 60, 64, 64] sts.
Rows 1–8: *K2, p2; rep from * to end.
Row 15 [RS]: Knit, inc 3 [3, 3, 2, 2] sts evenly across. 63 [63, 63, 66, 66] sts.
Row 16:
Sizes S, M, and L: P1 (edge st), *p5, k2; rep from * to last 6 sts, p5, p1 (edge st)
Sizes XL and 2XL: P1 (edge st), p3, k2, *p5, k2; rep from * to last 4 sts, p3, p1 (edge st).
Row 17: Knit.

Continue in garter rib as set, work 7 rows even.
Inc row [RS]: K1, m1, knit to last st, m1, k1. 2 sts inc'd.
Rep Inc Row on every 10th row 3 [5, 7, 7, 11] times more, then on every 14th row 2 [4, 3, 3, 1] times. Work increased sts into garter rib pattern. 75 [83, 85, 88, 92] sts.
Work even until sleeve measures 19.5 [20, 20.5, 21, 21.5]"/49.5 [51, 52, 53.5, 54.5]cm, ending with a WS row.

Bind off 8 [8, 8, 10, 10] sts at beg of next two rows. 59 [67, 69, 68, 72] sts. Place sts on waste yarn and set aside.

Yoke
All pieces are put on circular needle and yoke is worked flat in rows. Keep 1 st at each end as an edge st, worked in stockinette. Continue working color stripe pattern as established. Color stripe will migrate from front of sweater to left sleeve. Do not carry stripe pattern onto back of sweater. Vertical stripes on sleeves are started more closely together, 6 rows after previous one has been started. When working color stripe near and at the raglan decreases, work stripe for as long as possible, decreasing so that the stripe becomes the second to the last st before or after the stitch marker. If, due to decreasing, a stripe cannot be knit for long enough such that it is time to start the next stripe, simply start the next stripe once the previous one disappears.

With right sides facing, place on long circular needle the back, pm, first sleeve, pm, front, pm, second sleeve. 282 [312, 330, 334, 356] sts. Do not join.
Row 1 [RS]: Knit.
Row 2 [WS]: Work sts as they appear (knit the knits, purl the purls, work stripes as established).
Row 3 [dec row]: K2 (first st is edge st), k2tog, (knit to 3 sts before marker, ssk, k1, sl marker, k1, k2tog) three times, knit to last 4 sts, ssk, k2 (last st is edge st). 8 sts dec'd.
Work Rows 2–3 a total of 24 [26, 28, 28, 30] times. 90 [104, 106, 110, 116] sts.

Next row [WS]: Work sts as they appear, dec 2 [0, 2, 2, 0] sts evenly spaced. 88 [104, 104, 108, 116] sts rem.
Collar
Rows 1–14: *K2, p2; rep from * to end. If a sleeve stripe falls naturally into either a k2 or p2 column, you may choose to continue this stripe into the collar. Discontinue any other stripes.
Row 15 [RS]: Work in patt, dec by p2tog [6, 8, 8, 9, 9] p2 sections evenly around. 82 [96, 96, 99, 107] sts.
Rows 16–18: Work sts as they appear.
Bind off loosely in pattern.

FINISHING
Sew sides up to sleeves. Sew sleeves from cuff to underarm. Sew underarms closed. Sew back and sleeve together along raglan dec line and seam collar. Steam or wet block.

ABOUT THE DESIGNER
Nikki Adams has crocheted and knit for years, but has never successfully knit anything that her rabbit, Enif, has been willing to wear. Instead she enjoys knitting fur replacements for humans. Other hobbies include tending Gesneriads and buying fancy hair accessories. Find Nikki online as http://knitensity.blogspot.com and as mwedzi on Ravelry.com.

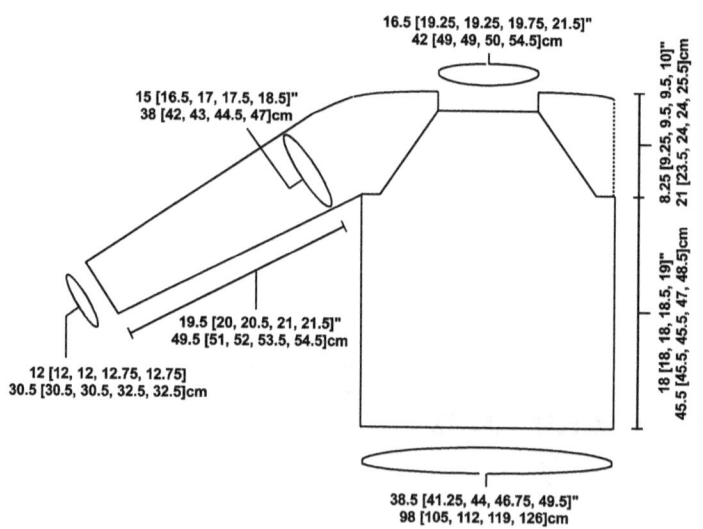

27

BRICK STITCH SCARF
BY REBEKAH BROMWELL

EASY

It's great fun seeing how various colors and tones in multi-layered stitch patterns work together. The raised garter stitch "mortar" in this pattern sets off the deeper background and gives an opportunity to use some gorgeous hand-dyed yarn to great effect. Vary how brightly colored your contrasting yarns are based on how adventurous the wearer is with their wardrobe!

SIZE
One size

FINISHED MEASUREMENTS
Width: 7"/18cm
Length: 75"/190cm

MATERIALS
Blue and gray scarf
[A] Flamboyance Yarns Bailey [100% Blue Faced Leicester wool; 181 yd/166m per 100g skein]; color Chinchilla; 1 skein
[B] Flamboyance Yarns Bailey; color Duck Egg; 1 skein

Red and gray scarf
[A] Indigodragonfly MCN Worsted [80% merino wool, 10% cashmere, 10% nylon; 180 yd/165m per 115g skein]; color Have Fun Stormin' the Castle; 1 skein
[B] Indigodragonfly MCN Worsted; color Rusty the Rooster; 1 skein

1 set US #6/4mm straight needles

GAUGE
17 sts/23 rows = 4"/10cm in pattern

PATTERN NOTES
This scarf can be knit to a length of 75"/190cm with just one skein of each color, but with a second skein of the B color you can have a particularly long and luxurious 107"/272cm scarf.

This pattern benefits greatly from blocking: the difference between the crumply pre-blocked fabric and silky drapey blocked stitches is remarkable.

PATTERN
With A, cast on 31 sts.
Row 1 [RS]: With A, knit.
Row 2 [WS]: With A, knit.
Row 3: With B, k1, (sl1 wyib, k3) 7 times, sl1, k1.
Row 4: With B, p1, (sl1 wyif, p3) 7 times, sl1, p1.
Row 5: With A, knit.
Row 6: With A, knit.
Row 7: With B, k3, (sl1 wyib, k3) 7 times.
Row 8: With B, p3, (sl1 wyif, p3) 7 times.
Rep Rows 1–8 until you're nearly out of yarn, or to desired length. Knit 3 rows with A. Bind off.

FINISHING
Weave in ends. Wash and lay flat to dry.

ABOUT THE DESIGNER
Rebekah's background in music, art, and engineering has led her to view knitting as a canvas not only for beautiful color and style, but mathematically elegant structure. A native New Yorker, she now knits and puzzles over efficient design in central Washington State surrounded by family, and beautiful mountain scenery. Find Rebekah online at http://seamlessknits.com, as @SeamlessKnits on Twitter, and FiberEscape on Ravelry.

BRIAN CARDIGAN

BY RUTH GARCIA-ALCANTUD

INTERMEDIATE

This design was inspired by my partner in crime, Brian, constant source of support and encouragement. The cables and rib will make any man look longer and leaner and will keep him warm in the middle of winter.

SIZE
S [M, L, XL, 2XL]
Shown in size M

FINISHED MEASUREMENTS
Chest: 36.5 [40, 44, 48.5, 52]"/92.5 [102, 112, 122.5, 132]cm
Length: 27.5 [29, 29.5, 30.5, 31]"/70.5 [74, 75, 77.5, 79]cm

MATERIALS
Spunky Eclectic Light Worsted Merino [100% merino wool; 500 yd/457m per 250g skein]; color Light Grey; 3 [3, 4, 4, 5] skeins

1 set US #7/4.5mm straight needles

Cable needle (cn)
Waste yarn or stitch holders
Sewing needle and coordinating thread
Separating zipper 28 [30, 30, 30, 30]"/71 [76, 76, 76, 76]cm long

GAUGE
23 sts/30 rows = 4"/10cm in stockinette

PATTERN NOTES
Note on gauge: Knitters' gauge varies greatly when working stockinette, rib, or cable. For clarification purposes, the blocked width of the Twist Cable at its narrowest is 2"/5cm, and for the Column Cable is 1.75"/4.5cm throughout. Work a big gauge swatch, as the garment's weight and the pull of the cables may change your gauge dramatically. Cable charts and garment schematics appear on pp. 33–35.

The cast on of choice for this pattern is the cable cast on. It allows the ribbing to look great while retaining an elasticity required for blocking and fitting.

STITCH INSTRUCTIONS
Wrap & turn: Wyib, sl next st pwise. Bring yarn to front. Return slipped st to LH needle. Turn work.
When you encounter a wrapped stitch on a subsequent row, you may pick up and knit or purl the wrap together with its stitch, if desired. Usually knit stitches look best if you do; purl stitches can go either way.

PATTERN
Left Front
Using the cable method, cast on 53 [58, 64, 70, 75] sts.
Row 1 [RS]: K6 [8, 8, 12, 13], p3 [3, 3, 5, 6], k9, p3 [3, 4, 4, 4], k3 [3, 4, 4, 4], p3 [3, 4, 4, 4], (k3, p2) three times, k3, p2 [3, 4, 4, 5], k2 [3, 4, 4, 5], p2 [3, 4, 4, 5], k2.
Row 2 [WS]: Work sts as they appear (knit the knits and purl the purls).
Rep Rows 1–2 twice more.

Pattern set-up row [RS]: K6 [8, 8, 12, 13], p3 [3, 3, 5, 6], work Row 1 of Column Cable Left, p3 [3, 4, 4, 4], k3 [3, 4, 4, 4], p3 [3, 4, 4, 4], work Row 1 of Twist Cable Left, p2 [3, 4, 4, 5], k2 [3, 4, 4, 5], p2 [3, 4, 4, 5], k2.
Pattern set-up row [WS]: Work sts as they appear, following Row 2 on both cable charts.
Continue as set by last two rows until work measures 17.25 [18, 18, 18.5, 18.5]"/44 [45.5, 45.5, 47, 47]cm from cast on, ending with a WS row.

Shape armhole
Bind off 3 [3, 3, 4, 4] sts at beg of next row [RS]. Work WS row even.
Bind off 1 [1, 2, 3, 4] sts at beg of next row. Work WS row even.
Bind off 1 [1, 2, 3, 3] sts at beg of next row. Work WS row even.
Bind off 1 [1, 1, 3, 3] sts at beg of next row. Work WS row even.
Bind off 0 [0, 1, 1, 2] sts at beg of next row. Work WS row even.
47 [52, 55, 56, 59] sts.
Size 2XL only: Dec 1 st at beg of next 2 RS rows. 57 sts.

Work even until armhole measures 9 [9.5, 10, 10.5, 11]"/23 [24.5, 25.5, 26.5, 28]cm, ending with a WS row.

Shape shoulders
Bind off 5 sts at beg of foll 3 [3, 4, 4, 5] RS rows. Work WS row even.
Bind off 4 [4, 4, 4, 4] sts at beg of next row. Work WS row even.
Bind off 3 [4, 4, 4, 0] sts at beg of next row. Work WS row even. (For size 2XL, skip these 2 rows.)
Size M only: Bind off 2 sts at beg of next row. Work WS row even.

Cut yarn leaving a long tail, slip rem 25 [27, 27, 28, 28] sts on to waste yarn or stitch holder and set aside.

Right Front
Using the cable method, cast on 53 [58, 64, 70, 75] sts.
Row 1 [RS]: K2, p2 [3, 4, 4, 5], k2 [3, 4, 4, 5], p2 [3, 4, 4, 5], k3, (p2, k3) three times, p3 [3, 4, 4, 4], k3 [3, 4, 4, 4], p3 [3, 4, 4, 4], k9, p3 [3, 5, 6], k6 [8, 8, 12, 13].
Row 2 [WS]: Work sts as they appear (knit the knits and purl the purls).
Rep Rows 1–2 twice more.

Pattern set-up row [RS]: K2, p2 [3, 4, 4, 5], k2 [3, 4, 4, 5], p2 [3, 4, 4, 5], work Row 1 of Twist Cable Right, p3 [3, 4, 4, 4], k3 [3, 4, 4, 4], p3 [3, 4, 4, 4], work Row 1 of Column Cable Right, p3 [3, 5, 6], k6 [8, 8, 12, 13].
Pattern set-up row [WS]: Work sts as they appear, following Row 2 on both cable charts.
Continue as for Left Front, reversing shaping by working all armhole bind offs and decreases and shoulder bind offs at the beginning of WS rows.

Back
Using the cable method, cast on 104 [116, 128, 140, 150] sts.
Row 1 (RS): K6 [8, 8, 12, 13], p3 [3, 3, 5, 6], k9, p3 [3, 4, 4, 4], k3 [3, 4, 4, 4], p3 [3, 4, 4, 4], k0 [2, 3, 3, 4], p0 [2, 2, 2, 4], (k3, p2) three times, k3, p5 [5, 6, 6, 6], k4 [4, 6, 6, 6], p5 [5, 6, 6, 6], (k3, p2) three times, k3, p0 [2, 2, 2, 4], k0 [2, 3, 3, 4], p3 [3, 4, 4, 4], k3 [3, 4, 4, 4], p3 [3, 4, 4, 4], k9, p3 [3, 3, 5, 6], k6 [8, 8, 12, 13].
Row 2 [WS]: Work sts as they appear (knit the knits and purl the purls).
Rep Rows 1–2 twice more.

Pattern set-up row [RS]: K6 [8, 8, 12, 13], p3 [3, 3, 5, 6], work Row 1 of Column Cable Right, p3 [3, 4, 4, 4], k3 [3, 4, 4, 4], p3 [3, 4, 4, 4], k0 [2, 3, 3, 4], p0 [2, 2, 2, 4], work Row 1 of Twist Cable Right, p5 [5, 6, 6, 6], k4 [4, 6, 6, 6], p5 [5, 6, 6, 6], work Row 1 of Twist Cable Left, p0 [2, 2, 2, 4], k0 [2, 3, 3, 4], p3 [3, 4, 4, 4], k3 [3, 4, 4, 4], p3 [3, 4, 4, 4], work Row 1 of Column Cable Left, p3 [3, 3, 5, 6], k6 [8, 8, 12, 13].
Pattern set-up row [WS]: Work sts as they appear, following Row 2 on cable charts.
Continue as set by last 2 rows until work measures 17.25 [18, 18, 18.5, 18.5]"/44 [45.5, 45.5, 47, 47]cm from cast on, ending with a WS row.

Shape armholes
Bind off 3 [3, 3, 4, 4] sts at the beg of next 2 rows.
Bind off 1 [1, 2, 3, 4] sts at the beg of next 2 rows.
Bind off 1 [1, 2, 3, 3] sts at the beg of next 2 rows.
Bind off 1 [1, 1, 3, 3] sts at the beg of next 2 rows.
Bind off 0 [0, 1, 1, 2] sts at the beg of next 2 rows. 92 [104, 110, 112, 118] sts.
Size 2XL only: Dec 1 st at the beg of the next 4 rows. 114 sts.
Work even until armholes measure 9 [9.5, 10, 10.5, 11]"/23 [24.5, 25.5, 26.5, 28]cm, ending with a WS row.

Shape shoulders and neck
Bind off 5 sts at the beg of the next 4 [6, 6, 6, 6] rows. 72 [74, 80, 82, 84] sts.
Next row [RS]: Bind off 5 [4, 5, 5, 5] sts, work until there are 23 [23, 26, 27, 28] sts on RH needle, turn. Slip rem 44 [47, 49, 50, 51] unworked sts to a holder.
Work WS row even.
Next row: Bind off 4 [4, 4, 4, 5] sts, work until there are 11 [10, 13, 13, 14] sts on RH needle, wrap & turn.
Work WS row even.
Next row: Bind off 3 [2, 4, 4, 4] sts. Cut yarn leaving a long tail and fasten off, leaving 16 [17, 18, 19, 19] live sts on a different stitch holder for neck.

Replace 44 [47, 49, 50, 51] held sts on needles. Join yarn with RS facing and work to end.
Next row [WS]: Bind off 5 [4, 5, 5, 5] sts, work until there are 15 [15, 17, 18, 18] sts on RH needle, wrap & turn.
Work RS row even.
Next row: Bind off 4 [4, 4, 4, 5] sts, work until there are 3 [2, 4, 4, 4] sts on RH needle, wrap & turn.
Work RS row even.
Next row: Bind off 3 [2, 4, 4, 4] sts. Cut yarn and fasten off. Add all 32 [37, 36, 37, 37] live sts to neck stitch holder.

Sleeve (Left)
Using the cable method, cast on 66 [72, 72, 72, 72] sts.
Row 1 [RS]: K2 [3, 3, 3, 3], p7 [8, 8, 8, 8], k8 [8, 8, 8, 8], p7 [8, 8, 8, 8], (k3, p2) three times, k3, p7 [8, 8, 8, 8], k8 [8, 8, 8, 8], p7 [8, 8, 8, 8], k2 [3, 3, 3, 3].
Row 2 [WS]: Work sts as they appear (knit the knits and purl the purls).

Pattern set-up row [RS]: K2 [3, 3, 3, 3], p7 [8, 8, 8, 8], k8 [8, 8, 8, 8], p7 [8, 8, 8, 8], work Row 1 of Twist Cable Left, p7 [8, 8, 8, 8], k8 [8, 8, 8, 8], p7 [8, 8, 8, 8], k2 [3, 3, 3, 3].

Pattern set-up row [WS]: Work sts as they appear, working Row 2 of Twist Cable Left.
Continue as set by last two rows for a further 4 rows.
Inc row [RS]: K1, m1, work to last st, m1, k1. 2 sts inc'd.
Cont in patt, rep Inc Row on every 8th [8th, 10th, 10th, 8th] row 5 [5, 11, 13, 16] times more. 78 [84, 96, 100, 106] sts.
Work even until sleeve measures 18 [18.5, 19.5, 20, 20.5]"/45.5 [47, 49.5, 51, 52]cm, ending with a WS row.
Shape cap
Note: Do not work cabling (chart rows 15–28) on sleeve cap unless a cable is already underway. If this is the case, finish the cable sequence and stop working cable at that point.
Bind off 3 [3, 3, 4, 4] sts at the beg of next 2 rows.
Bind off 1 [1, 2, 3, 4] sts at the beg of next 2 rows.
Bind off 1 [1, 2, 3, 3] sts at the beg of next 2 rows.
Bind off 1 [1, 1, 3, 3] sts at the beg of next 2 rows.
Bind off 0 [0, 1, 1, 2] sts at the beg of next 2 rows. (If number is 0, omit these rows.) 66 [72, 78, 72, 74] sts.
Bind off 2 [2, 2, 1, 1] sts at the beg of next 18 [20, 22, 26, 26] rows.
Bind off 1 [1, 1, 2, 2] sts at the beg of next 2 [2, 2, 6, 6] rows.
Bind off 3 sts at beg of next 4 rows.
Bind off rem 16 [18, 20, 22, 24] sts.

Sleeve (right)
Work as for Left Sleeve, using Twist Cable Right.

FINISHING
Pin out the garment pieces to schematic measurements and steam block to encourage fiber bloom and allow the cables to pop. When dry, seam up the fronts and back at the shoulders.

Zipper
Lay garment flat and pin the bottom of the zipper to the bottom of the garment. Working on both sides at the same time to ensure the zipper lies flat and does not create any bumps on the fabric, pin evenly all the way to the top. If there's any extra length on the zipper, fold and pin towards the inside of the garment. With matching thread and needle, backstitch with small stitches, working from the RS. If required, work a second line of stitches to secure inner edge of zipper to the garment.

Collar
With RS facing and starting on the Right Front, pick up all the held sts around the neck area from the Right Front, Back and Left Front, and work in pattern as they appear, NOT working cables. Work stitches as they appear, back and forth in rows until collar measures 4.5"/11cm or desired length. Bind off in pattern.

Seam up the sides of the fronts to the back, and sleeve seams. Set the sleeves in, easing in any fullness as you work.

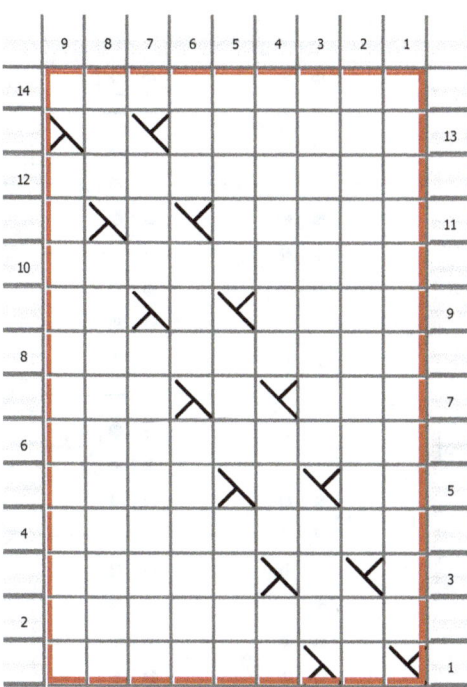

COLUMN CABLE LEFT CHART

c2 over 1 left
RS: sl2 to CN, hold in front. k1, k2 from CN
WS: sl2 to CN, hold in front. k1, k2 from CN

knit
RS: knit stitch
WS: purl stitch

purl
RS: purl stitch
WS: knit stitch

c2 over 1 right
RS: sl1 to CN, hold in back. k2, k1 from CN
WS: sl1 to CN, hold in back. k2, k1 from CN

C3 over 5 right
RS: Sl 5 to cn and hold to back, k3, [p2, k3] from cn.
WS:

C3 over 5 left
RS: Sl 3 to cn and hold to front, k3, p2, k3 from cn.
WS:

TWIST CABLE LEFT CHART TWIST CABLE RIGHT CHART

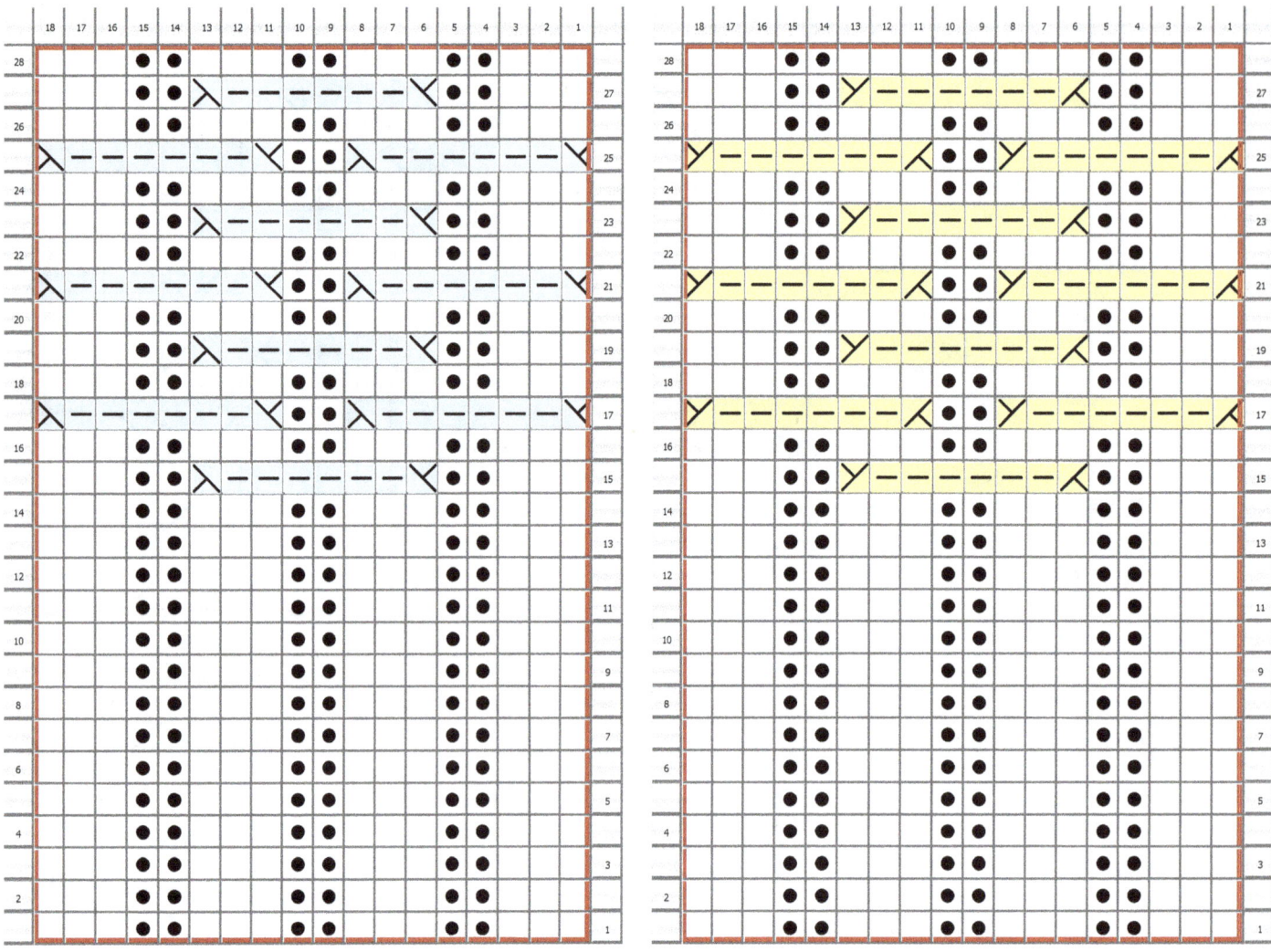

ABOUT THE DESIGNER
Ruth plays with yarn and fiber from her home in Sussex, UK. She loves to design with small details and bright colors to create a timeless wardrobe. Visit her at http://www.rockandpurl.com or on Ravelry as rockandpurl.

COLUMN CABLE RIGHT CHART

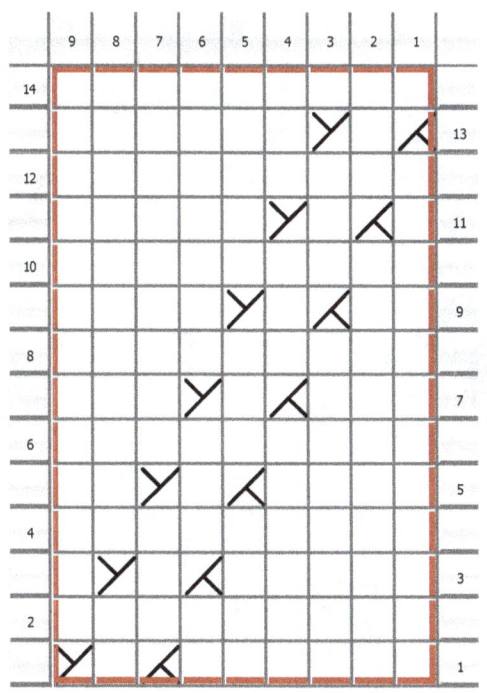

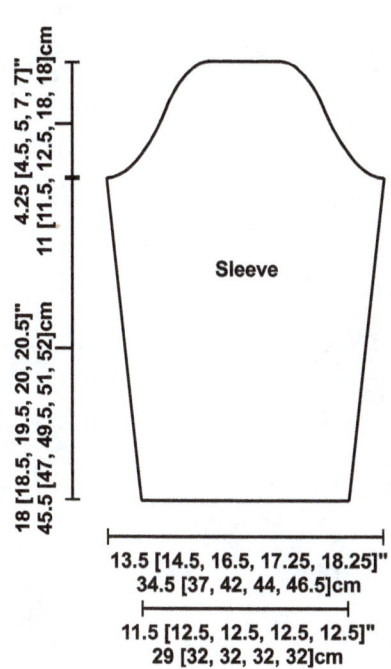

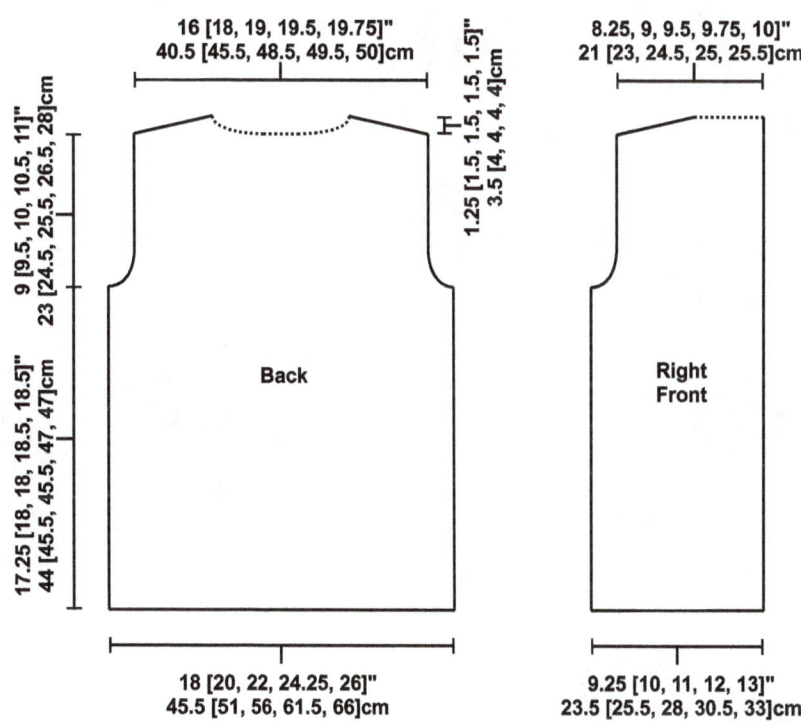

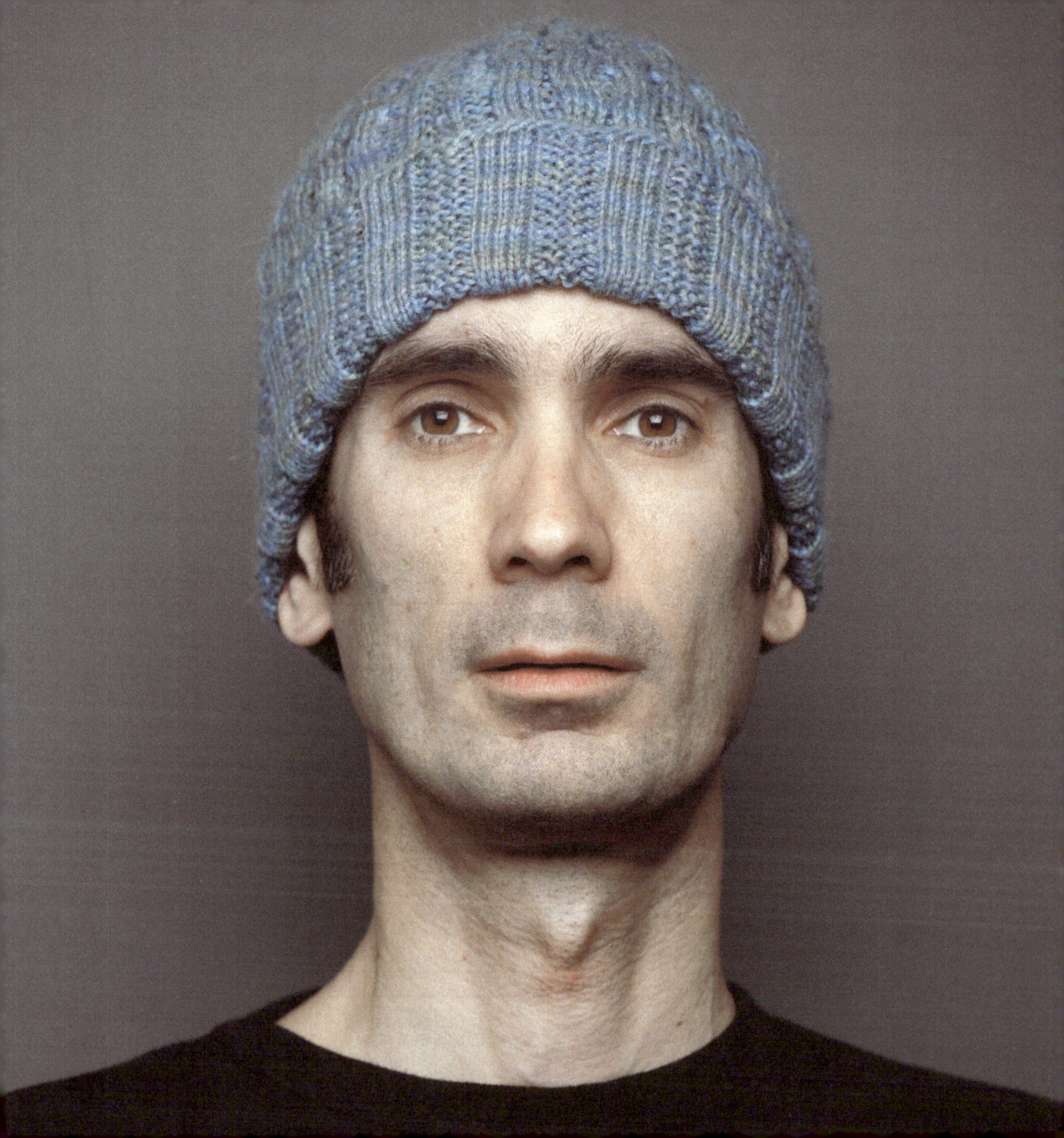

ABALONE COVE HAT
BY STEPHANNIE TALLENT

EXPERIENCED

The decreasing honeycomb cables of this hat remind me of the rocks at Abalone Cove, Palos Verdes Peninsula, a wonderful place to go tidepooling.

FINISHED MEASUREMENTS
Circumference (unstretched): 17"/43cm
Height (including ribbing): 12"/30.5cm

MATERIALS
Spirit Trail Fiberworks Lyra [50% alpaca, 30% merino, 20% silk; 400 yd per 183g skein]; color Blue Jeans; 1 skein. Hat as written takes approx. 225 yd/205m.

1 set US #3/3.25mm double pointed needles, or 32"/80cm circular for Magic Loop
1 set US #4/3.5mm double pointed needles, or 32"/80cm circular for Magic Loop

Stitch marker(s)
Cable needle (cn)

GAUGE
32 sts/38 rows = 4"/10cm in pattern ribbing with smaller needles

PATTERN
Ribbing
Using smaller needles, cast on 128 sts. Join in the round, being careful not to twist. Place marker for beg of rnd.

Rnd 1: *K4, p4; rep from * to end.
Rnd 2: *K1, p1, k2, p4; rep from * to end.
Rnd 3: *K2, p1, k1, p4; rep from * to end.
Rep Rnds 2–3 until ribbing measures 5in/12.5cm, ending with Rnd 3.

Crown
Work following Chart to end. The chart pattern is repeated 4 times per round. Place markers between repeats if desired.

FINISHING
Cut yarn, draw through 8 remaining stitches to close top of hat. Weave in loose ends. Block if desired.

ABOUT THE DESIGNER
Stephannie lives in Hermosa Beach, California, with husband Dave, dog Rigel and Tonkinese cats Meggie, Obi and Cali. When she's not designing, knitting or working as a veterinarian, she gardens (native plants and vegetables), hikes, and beachcombs. She blogs at www.sunsetcat.com and you can find her as Stephcat on Ravelry. Don't miss her Cooperative Press book *California Revival Knits*!

38

Symbol	Name	Description
□	**knit**	knit stitch
⊡	**purl**	purl stitch
■	**No Stitch**	Placeholder - No stitch made.
M	**make one**	Make one by lifting strand in between stitch just worked and the next stitch, knit into back of this thread.
	c4 over 2 right P	sl2 to CN, hold in back. k4, then p2 from CN
	c4 over 2 left P	sl4 to CN, hold in front. p2, then k4 from CN
	3/2 LC with SSK and purl background	Slip 4 sts to CN, hold to front. P2. K1, ssk, k1 from CN.
	3/2 RC with k2tog and purl background	Slip 2 sts to CN, hold to back. K1, k2tog, k1, p2 from CN.
■	**No Stitch**	Placeholder - No stitch made.
	p2tog	Purl 2 stitches together
	c3 over 1 right P	sl1 to CN, hold in back. k3, p1 from CN
	c3 over 1 left P	sl3 to CN, hold in front. p1, k3 from CN
	2/1 LC with SSK and purl background	Slip 3 sts to CN, hold in front. P1. SSK, k1 from CN.
	2/1 RC with k2tog and purl background	Slip 1 st to CN, hold in back. K2tog, k1. P1 from CN.
	c2 over 1 right P	sl1 to CN, hold in back. k2, p1 from CN
	c2 over 1 left P	sl2 to CN, hold in front. p1, k2 from CN
	1/1 LC with ssk and purl background	Sl 2 to CN. P1. SSK from CN.

RIGA SWEATER
BY SUSANNA FERGUSON

EXPERIENCED

This sweater is knitted entirely in the round with saddle shoulders and a crew neck. A Latvian braid creates a distinctive hem and cuffs, while the slip-stitch stripe pattern on the body is simple yet graphic. The overall effect is sculptural but spare.

SIZES
S [M, L, XL, 2XL]
Shown in size S

FINISHED MEASUREMENTS
Chest: 40.5 [43, 45.5, 48, 50.5]"/103 [109, 115.5, 122, 128]cm
Length: 27 [28, 29, 29.75, 30.5]"/68.5 [71, 73.5, 75.5, 77.5]cm

MATERIALS
[MC] Debbie Bliss Cashmerino Aran [55% merino wool, 33% microfiber, 12% cashmere; 100yd/90m per 50g skein]; color #004 navy; 7 [8, 8, 9, 10] skeins
[CC] Debbie Bliss Cashmerino Aran; color #009 gray; 6 [7, 7, 8, 9] skeins

1 set US #8/5mm double pointed needles
1 set US #9/5.5mm double pointed needles
32"/80cm US #9/5.5mm circular needle

Stitch markers
Removable markers
Cable needle (cn)

GAUGE
19 sts/24 rows = 4"/10cm in swallow pattern with larger needles
16 sts/24 rows = 4"/10cm in stockinette with larger needles

STITCH INSTRUCTIONS
2-Color Rib (multiple of 2 sts)
Rnd 1: With MC, knit.
Rnd 2: With MC, *k1, p1; rep from * to end.
Rnd 3: With CC, knit.
Rnd 4: With CC, *k1, p1; rep from * to end.
Rep Rnds 1–4.

Latvian Braid
Set-up rnd: *K1 with MC, k1 with CC; rep from * to end.
Rnd 1: *With both yarns in front of work, p1 with MC, then p1 with CC; rep from * to end of rnd. Always bring working yarn UNDER the other; yarns will twist on this row, but untwist on the next.
Rnd 2: *With both yarns in front of work, p1 with MC, then p1 with CC; rep from * to end of rnd. Always bring working yarn OVER the other.
Rep Rnds 1–2.

Swallow Pattern
RST (right slipped twist) Sl next st to cn and hold to back of work, k1, sl st from cn to RH needle without working it.

LST (left slipped twist) Sl next st to cn and hold to front of work, sl 1 st to RH needle without working it, k1 from cn.

Set-up rnds 1 & 2: With MC, *k5, sl2, k5; rep from * to end.
Pattern rnd 1: With CC, *k4, RST, LST, k4; rep from * to end.
Pattern rnd 2: With CC, *k5, sl2, k5; rep from * to end.
Pattern rnd 3: With MC, *k4, RST, LST, k4; rep from * to end.
Pattern rnd 4: With MC, *k5, sl2, k5; rep from * to end.
Rep Pattern Rnds 1–4.

Striped Stockinette
Rnds 1–2: Knit with CC.
Rnds 3–4: Knit with MC.
Rep Rnds 1–4.

RLI (right lifted increase) Insert the tip of the RH needle into the left side of the st 1 row below the next st on the LH needle and knit into it.
LLI (left lifted increase) Insert the tip of the LH needle into the right side of the st 2 rows below the last st on the RH needle and knit into it.

PATTERN NOTES
Marked stitches: All yoke decreases will include marked stitches. When working ssk, k2tog, or p2tog with a marked stitch, always replace the marker in the resulting stitch. Beginning of round occurs at a marked stitch so be sure to adjust tension on color change rows and not let the yarns loosen too much.

Working jogless stripes: On color change rnd, lift the stitch below the first stitch of the round onto the left needle and knit it together with the first stitch of the round.

PATTERN
Body
With MC and circular needle, cast on 170 [180, 190, 200, 210] sts, pm and join for knitting in the round. Knit 1 rnd. Work Latvian Braid three times. Knit 1 rnd.
Next rnd: Knit, inc 22 [24, 26, 28, 30] sts evenly spaced. 192 [204, 216, 228, 240] sts.
Begin working Swallow Pattern. On first rnd, place a second marker after 96 [102, 108, 114, 120] sts. Work even in patt until body measures 17.5 [18.5, 19, 19, 19.5]"/44.5 [47, 48, 48, 50]cm, ending with Rnd 3 of pattern.
Next rnd: Bind off 7 [7, 8, 8, 8] sts, work in patt to 7 [7, 8, 8, 8] sts before second marker, bind off 14 [14, 16, 16, 16] sts, work in patt to last 7 [7, 8, 8, 8] sts, bind off 7 [7, 8, 8, 8] sts. Break yarns and set body aside.

Sleeves
With MC and larger dpn, cast on 32 [34, 38, 40, 42] sts. Pm and join for knitting in the round. Knit 1 rnd. Work Latvian Braid once. Change to smaller dpn and work Rnds 1–4 of 2-Color Rib Pattern three times, then Rnds 1–2 once more. Change to larger dpn and work in Striped Stockinette. Inc 2 sts on every 6th rnd 13 [12, 12, 13, 13] times as foll: K1, LLI, work to last st, RLI, k1. 58 [58, 62, 66, 68] sts. Work even until sleeve measures 20.5 [21, 22, 23, 24]"/52 [53, 56, 58.5, 61]cm, ending with Rnd 3 of stripe patt.
Next rnd: Bind off 7 [7, 8, 8, 8] sts, knit to last 7 [7, 8, 8, 8] sts, bind off 7 [7, 8, 8, 8] sts. Break yarns.

Yoke
Join sleeves to body
Attach MC to first sleeve and with circular needle, knit 44 [44, 46, 50, 52] sleeve sts, then work in pattern across 82 [88, 92, 98, 104] back sts, placing removable markers in first and last back sts. Knit 44 [44, 46, 50, 52] sleeve sts, then knit 82 [88, 92, 98, 104] front sts, placing removable markers in first and last front sts. 252 [264, 276, 296, 312] sts.

Round now begins at front right sleeve. Be sure to adjust tension here on color change rounds. Throughout yoke, continue in Swallow Pattern over body sections and Striped Stockinette over sleeve sections.

Work even for 1 [1, 1.25, 1.5, 1.5]"/2.5 [2.5, 3, 4, 4]cm.

Body dec rnd: *Work to marked st, ssk, work to 1 st before marked st, k2tog; repeat from * once more. 4 sts dec'd. The last k2tog is also the first stitch of the next round, so when dec falls on a color change rnd work the dec in the new color.
Rep Body Dec Rnd 5 [5, 5, 6, 6] times more. 228 [240, 252, 268, 284] sts.

Sleeve dec rnd: *Ssk, work to 1 st before marked st, k2tog; repeat from * once more. 4 sts dec'd.
Rep Sleeve Dec Rnd 14 [14, 15, 17, 18] times more. 14 sts rem in each sleeve section; 168 [180, 188, 196, 208] sts in total.

Work Body Dec Rnd 10 times. 128 [140, 148, 156, 168] sts rem; 50 [56, 60, 64, 70] in back and front sections, and 14 in each sleeve. Change from circular needle to dpn when necessary.

Saddles
Row 1 [RS]: Work across 14 sleeve sts to marked st, ssk, turn.
Row 2 [WS]: Sl1, work to marked st, p2tog, turn.
Row 3: Sl1, work to marked st, ssk, turn.
Rep Rows 2–3 7 [8, 9, 10, 12] times more, then Row 2 once more.

Work across back sts to second sleeve and complete saddle as for first sleeve. Work to beg of rnd. 92 [100, 104, 108, 112] sts.

Neck shaping
The neck is shaped with short rows.
Row 1 [RS]: Knit across saddle to marked st, ssk, work across back to 1 st before marked st, k2tog, knit across saddle to next marked st, ssk, turn.
Row 2 [WS]: Sl1, work back to marked st at beg of rnd, p2tog.
Rows 3–4: Rep Rows 1–2. 8 sts dec'd.
Row 5: Knit across saddle to marked st, ssk, work across back to 1 st before marked st, k2tog, turn. 2 sts dec'd.
Row 6: Sl1, work across back to 1 st before marked st, p2tog, turn. 1 st dec'd.
Row 7: Sl1, work across back to 1 st before marked st, k2tog. Do not turn. 1 st dec'd.
80 [88, 92, 96, 100] sts rem.

Neckband
With MC and smaller dpn, working fairly tightly, work k1, p1 rib over all sts for 4 rnds. Bind off loosely in rib.

FINISHING
Weave in all ends. Sew bound-off stitches at underarms together. Block to measurements and press lightly. The slip stitch pattern evens out nicely with blocking and pressing.

ABOUT THE DESIGNER
Susi Ferguson is a passionate runner, mother of three and artist. She is always accompanied by her Hungarian pointer Ginny and sometimes by her patient husband on the trails of the mountains of southern Germany where she lives.

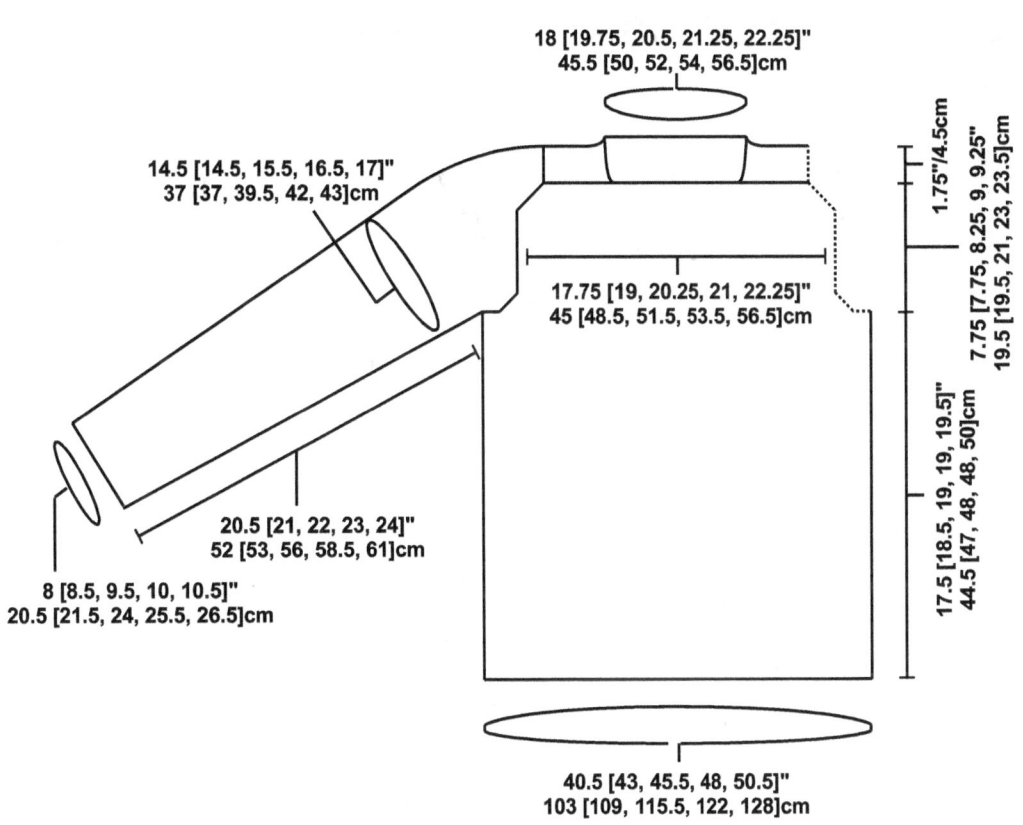

ACKNOWLEDGMENTS

Thank you to the designers who created such beautiful work for the book. Our biggest thanks to photographer Robert Gladys, makeup artist Elle Gemma, and to our models Ben Vendetta, Arabella Proffer and Chris McKay, as well as to Abra Forman, whose considerable talents helped bring the project together in its early stages. Sarah Jo Burch helped keep things running so Abra and Shannon could get things done, and MJ Kim did a massive amount of organizational work before we handed everything off to the talented technical editor, Alexandra Virgiel. Elizabeth Green Musselman came late to the team but helped enormously with wrapping up loose ends.

The book wouldn't be nearly as beautiful without the yarns contributed by the companies below.

We'd also like to thank the generous patrons whose Kickstarter support helped make this book series possible.

• •

YARNS FEATURED IN THIS BOOK:

Pigeonroof Studios (http://www.etsy.com/shop/pigeonroofstudios)
Three Irish Girls (http://www.threeirishgirls.com)
Hemp for Knitting (http://www.hempforknitting.com)
Ambrosia and Bliss (http://www.etsy.com/shop/AmbrosiaandBliss)
Flamboyance Yarns (http://flamboyanceyarns.co.uk)
Indigodragonfly (http://www.indigodragonfly.ca)
Spunky Eclectic (http://www.spunkyeclectic.com)
Spirit Trail Fiberworks (http://www.spirit-trail.net)
Debbie Bliss (http://www.debbieblissonline.com)

ABOUT COOPERATIVE PRESS

partners in publishing

Cooperative Press (formerly anezka media) was founded in 2007 by Shannon Okey, a voracious reader as well as writer and editor, who had been doing freelance acquisitions work, introducing authors with projects she believed in to editors at various publishers.

Although working with traditional publishers can be very rewarding, there are some books that fly under their radar. They're too avant-garde, or the marketing department doesn't know how to sell them, or they don't think they'll sell 50,000 copies in a year.

5,000 or 50,000. Does the book matter to that 5,000? Then it should be published.

In 2009, Cooperative Press changed its named to reflect the relationships we have developed with authors working on books. We work together to put out the best quality books we can, and share in the proceeds accordingly.

Thank you for supporting independent publishers and authors.

We're on Ravelry as CooperativePress. Please join our low-volume mailing list and check out our other books at…

HTTP://WWW.COOPERATIVEPRESS.COM

ABOUT FRESH DESIGNS

Shannon Okey wanted to do something to showcase emerging design talent after she left the editorship of a UK print knitting magazine; Fresh Designs is the result. A partnership between talented designers and primarily small/indie yarn companies (all of whom are thanked on the previous page — please help support these remarkable companies when you next shop for yarn), the first 10 Fresh Designs books have also broken the mold for designer compensation. Each time you purchase a Fresh Designs book or pattern, the designers receive a royalty share. We hope you'll enjoy meeting the designers in these pages, and that you'll check out the other books in the Fresh Designs series.

ABBREVIATIONS

alt	alternate
approx	approximately
beg	begin/beginning
BO	bind off
CC	contrasting color
cn	cable needle
CO	cast on
dec	decrease(s)/decreasing
dpn	double pointed needle
est	established
foll	follows/following
inc	increase(s)/increasing
k	knit
k2tog	knit 2 together
kfb	knit into the front and back of the same stitch
kwise	knitwise
LH	left hand
m1	make 1 stitch
M1L	make 1 left
M1R	make 1 right
MC	main color
p	purl
patt	pattern
pm	place marker
p2tog	purl 2 together
psso	pass slipped st over
pwise	purlwise
rem	remain/remaining
rep(s)	repeat(s)
RH	right hand
rnd(s)	round(s)
RS	right side
sl	slip
ssk	slip, slip, knit these 2 sts together
tbl	through the back loop
tog	together
WS	wrong side
wyib	with yarn in back
wyif	with yarn in front
yo	yarn over